Trisanne's Unspoken Truth

Trisanne's Unspoken Truth

A Story of Triumph Over Adversity

Trisanne Morris

CONTENTS

INTRODUCTION

My name is Trish, I'm a lovely soul to meet

I am a proud Cancer, born to be unique.

A proud mom to a handsome baby boy who is so dear,

A recent divorcée, with a story you might wanna hear.

My style is edgy, with just a tiny flair,

Red and black outfits, with silver or gold to spare.

I enjoy singing, signing and writing poetry too,

But spending time with my little one is what I mostly love
to do.

Life hasn't been easy, I have faced my fair share

Of heartbreak and challenges with absolutely no one to care.

As a former bisexual woman, I have found my way,

I have discovered my truth and come what may.

I've battled mental health, with its many ups and downs,

PTSD, depression and anxiety, just loves wearing my crown.

But I have found happiness in embracing my soul,

And being my true self is my ultimate goal.

I give off a dominant personality, but have a heart so bold,

Definitely weak for dominant femmes, with a love that's worth more than just any gold.

I value physical touch and words of affirmation too,

And if I commit, I'll be all in... that much I know is true

So if you're up for the challenge and willing to take a chance,

Let's see where this journey can take us and see if our love will enhance.

I may be difficult to love, but I am definitely worth the fight,

I love hard and I expect the same, all day and all night.

A New Chapter Unfolds

I feel like my life is finally starting to have some meaning

It's like I just wanna keep on dreaming

Finally feels like everything is coming into place

And I know that I deserve it, after everything I've had to face

2024 may not have been my year

After all the times I've cried, I don't wanna drop another tear

But 2025 sure will be my biggest comeback

Because if I've learnt anything, is that it was never anything I lack

People just know how to use and abuse

Which is why I won't be sharing my good news

Move in silence, celebrate aloud, right?

Because it's better to let people assume than to know what's in sight

So I'm gonna keep hope alive that I'm getting everything that's coming to me

And I won't ever stop until I'm fully happy and free

This coming year will be a year to remember

From January all the way to December

A Mother's Unbroken Spirit

I'll be okay

That is all I gotta say, right?

My struggles and pain will all be worth it

Bcz as much as I want to, I will not quit

My life may not have been a pot of gold

But my son has made my life feel complete and whole

I can never imagine not being there for him when he needs me most

Because our bond will always remain close

So for 2025, I'll bounce back better than ever

Because I'm not giving up, not ever

So yes, I know I'll be okay

It'll be my year, even if every day is not my day

Jamaica's Cry

I don't know what's going on with 2024

But this was not the year I was hoping for

I wanted peace, not pain

I wanted to cry, but not in vain

This year has probably been the worst year

Because every day, every week, every month, it's a different fear

Us Jamaicans have got to get it together

We're supposed to build together, not tear down each other

I am proud to be a Jamaican, don't get me wrong

But how many more ways are there left for us to have to be strong

I've hardly met a Jamaican that has had an easy life

It's either you're a broken child, broken mother or a broken wife

It's one death after the other

That's someone's son, grandson and brother

This year is a year we will never forget

And I hate that we now have to live every day, with a fret

THE WEIGHT OF EXISTENCE

This life doesn't feel like a life worth living

Because everyone keeps taking and not giving

I can't living like this, always waiting for the next shoe to drop

But it doesn't look like it is ever going to stop

Why can't I be normal? Why is it so hard?

It's like no matter what I play, it's never the right card

I'm tired bro. I'm genuinely getting tired

I'm starting to feel so uninspired

I need a break bro, I need a freaking break

Because everyone turns out to be a freaking fake

When is it ever gonna be my turn?

How many more lessons are there really left to learn?

Why did it have to be me?

Why can't I just be free?

This life really isn't a life worth living

Because everyone keeps taking and not giving

The 1% That Haunts Me

One day without anxiety is all I really ask for

Because all this fear keeps coming through my door

What am I afraid of? What's holding me back?

Is it because of something I lack?

The weight on my chest, the tingling in my brain

Is taking everything from me, I am so drained

I don't want to be om the stronger soldiers list anymore

Because it is getting no better than before

I just want to be free. To love without fear

But that'll never happen, starting to see that very clear

So I guess I'll get accustomed, accept that it's a part of my life, forever

And it'll never go away, not now, not ever

A Life Of Fear

Anxiety's grips is so tight, it's seriously a constant fight

There's always that far that's lurking. Day and endless night

I hate that I have to live with this weight

It's like I cant get a damn thigh straight

I wish I didn't know this kind of pain, this fear that is always so near

It's a constant reminder that I'm living in fear

It make my life feels like it's not worth living, like a never ending test

But I still push on because I know that I need to f]do my best

Just one day is all I ask for, a day without anxiety's grasp

A day to feel normal and be free at last

Is that too much to ask for? Can I get just one day of peace?

A day to live without this weight would be an amazing release

This pain is not a pain I'd wish on not even my worst enemy

This kind of pain is relentless, and can be hard to see

But still I will hold on to hope, a glimmer of light

Hoping for a chance to overcome and rise above this endless fight

Growth Through Struggles

2024, a year that has left it's marks

A year that was filled with struggles but also had a little spark

I wanted to give up so bad but I chose to stay and fight

In silence and aloud, I always stood up for what's right

I have come a long way and i am really proud to say

I'm happy and I actually meant it, in every single way

No more hiding, no more shame

I am a lesbian, and I am very proud, to proclaim

Being true to myself will always be the best thing I have
ever done

I am free to be me without the fear of being undone

This year has taught be that the darkness will pass

And the sun will shine again, and I'll be there, first cl;ass

I'm rising above because I know that I'm more than I need to be

I am strong, I am proud and I'm finally free

I know I've got this, I know I'll be just fine

I'm really happy, I'm me and I'm feeling so divine

Forever In My Heart

My beautiful aunt, gone too soon in May

Leaving me with just memories, right before Mother's Day

No more calls, no more laughter, no more beautiful delight

Your absence echos even more through these darkest nights

I miss hearing your singing, your beautiful voice so sweet

Filling my heart with joy, our moment to meet

Your daily company is missed because now just a memory stays

Wanting to be able to turn back time to relive all the sunny days

Christmas without you will never be the same

There's an empty chair, a silent room a very hallow pain

Your love, your light, your presence, is now gone

A void that echoes, where your warmth once shone

I'm still struggling to accept this unbearable loss

Your absence cuts deep, it's like an unhealing cross

How can I move on when with each step I take,

Keep reminding me of you, and the memories we would make?

Time may soften the edge but it won't erase

The ache of your leaving, the space you occupied

Your love remain like a flame that burns so bright

Guiding me through the darkness and into the light

Though you're no longer here, your legacy will still stays

In my heart, in my memories, on every sunny day

I'll hold on to these and cherish every moment we've shared

Forever in my heart, my beloved aunt, forever cared

Raising Above The Weight

Anxiety's heavyweight presses down on my chest,

It's a constant weight that brings me no rest.

The shaking, the tingling sensations in my brain so bright,

Tears flowing uncontrollably, day and endless night.

My stomach twists in knots, thoughts are entwined in fear,

Social anxiety binds me so silent and clear.

I'm afraid to speak first, the words tangled in my mind,

Afraid of judgment, rejection's chilling find.

Humiliation's specter looms, it's a constant and gnawing pain,

Rejection's shadow, a suffocating grip that refuses to wane.

I'm trapped in this labyrinth, still with no clear exit sign,

Anxiety's darkness holds my only guiding light, it's a constant whine.

I yearn for understanding, just for one a listening ear,

But it's hard to find solace, when no one's near.

I'm tired of pretending, of putting on this mask,

Hiding all my pain, all my fears, all my anxious tasks.

Anxiety follows me everywhere, it's a constant and gnawing weight,

A pain that's magnified by people who don't even understand my fate.

I'm surrounded by faces, that don't recognize my plight,

Leaving me feeling isolated, in this endless and darkest night.

I wish for peace, just for a calm and quiet night,

Free from the weight of anxiety's crushing might.

But until then, I'll keep holding on to hope's thin thread,

And search for strength, in every anxious dread.

Anxiety's definitely not something easy, to live with each day,

The more attacks I get, the closer it feels like I'm fading away.

I really hate this constant pain, that just refuses to subside,

It's a weight that's crushing me, with every anxious stride.

But I'll rise above and face my fears with might,

And shine a light on anxiety and bring it into sight.

For I know I am not alone, with this anxious fight,

And together we'll rise, into the light of hope and new sight.

A New Year's Wish

A huge Merry Christmas to my fellow friends and families
and I wish you a prosperous New Year

I know that this year and been a rough year for most of us,
with the drop of every tear

But those struggles are gonna lead to an even bigger cele-
bration

Because no matter how much times life knocks us down, we
always get up and take action

I'm praying for a the year of 2025 to be filled with joy and
laughter for each and every one of us

I pray there are more are more joy than fuss

Let us all try to bring each other up and now tear each
other down

Whether they're dark, white, yellow or brown

Let's laugh together, and be there for each other

Whether it's a father, aunt, uncle, daughter or brother

We're all one United family, by God

So let's live like one, even if we have a few flaws

All the struggles, pain and miseries will all be worth it

And no matter what life has in store for us, we will get up, shake off and not quit

So I know 2025 is gonna be a year that we'll all remember

From January all the way to December

A Hollow Soul

I'm so lost in this emptiness, it's a hollow space

Feeling nothing, it's just a numb and empty place

When I lost my best friend, I thought I'd feel some pain

But the numbness took over.. It's a never-ending rain

My mouth wanted to say more, to express my sorrow

But words wouldn't form into words and my heart felt hallow

I imagined speaking up but the silence took the stage

Leaving me with nothing; just a numb and empty page

I feel nothing; no joy, no tears, no fears

Just a dull emptiness that brings me to my knees through the years

Its just for my protection, to shield my heart from pain

But it's also pushing away the people that have been there, who care and remain

To those who stuck around, especially through my darkest nights

I really appreciate your love, your patience and your guiding lights

You help me feel less than alone, in this numb and empty space

And for that, I'll be forever grateful, for your love and gentle face

Treasured Friendship

We just met the energy I feel

Has never felt more real

A friend like you is hard to find

And honestly, I don't mind

You're a dope, funny dude with a heart of gold

I really love hanging with you because our vibes will never get old

You listen without judgement, a friendly ear

A safe space to talk without even a peak of fear

I really appreciate you more than words are enough to say

You're an amazing friend in every single way

I hope you know how much you and this friendship means
to me

A true friend like you is a treasure to see

Risen Above

I have risen above and I've made it through

The darkest of days even though the struggles? A few

My confidence is coming from rock bottom low

Now I stand tall with a heart that now glows

I love my life and my lifestyle, it's me to the core

It brings me peace and a sense of freedom galore

I wake up each day always with a smile so wide

Loving my job and the people by my side

For the first time in years, I can say with glee

"I'm really happy" and actually mean it, from the heart, wild and free

No more pretending, no more hiding the pain

I have found true happiness and I'm living again

My Anxiety

A weight upon my chest so tight

Its hard to breathe, whether day or night

I break down very easily, tears fall like rain

No reason why, it's a constant pain

When my hands shake, my heart does too

A never ending cycle but what to do?

It hurts me so much, this anxious strife

Its a burden to bear in this life

No one understands the pain I face

The weight of anxiety is a dark and lonely place

I really want to feel okay, to be set free

From the prison and fear of anxiety

I want to feel normal, even just for a day

To breathe without the weight, to drive the anxiety away

But till then, I'll keep holding on tight

And hope that someday, everything will be alright

Embracing My Truth

I wore the label "bisexual" with pride

But deep inside there was a truth that I couldn't hide

A year ago, I broke free from the chains

Embracing my heart and easing women's pains

Being straight was a phase, just a mask I wear

Being a lesbian is me, without a single care

No more pretending and hiding in fear

I am who I am and now my heart is clear

Homophobic voices tried to suppress

My love, my identity and my happiness

But I stood tall and refuse to conceal

M true self, my love, my heart's reveal

Now I can live the authentically, unapologetically me

Surrounded by love that sets me free

Those who truly matter accepts me with pride

No more hiding because I'm alive and I won't divide

A Tribute To True Friends

I've had these friends for four years

And they've been there with me through every tears

I really do not know what I would do without them

But to me, they're the greatest gem

They influenced me to leave my toxic marriage

Because they always thought I deserved more than average

And even though we might not talk everyday

I still love and appreciate them, even when I don't say

Thank you guys for making these 4 years not so hard

Making you guys my friends was definitely the right card

So I'm glad to be going into 2025 with you

And I wouldn't want it any other way, after all we've been through

Echoes In My Mind

The voices haunts me, they whispers loud and clear

"You're too big, too fat, it'll never disappear"

A chorus of shame and a symphony of pain

It's a struggle with each bite and every meal is a strain

I try to eat but these fears takes hold

Gaining weight, maybe growing old

My self esteem shattered, lost and worn

A reflection distorted, I'm forever torn

I've shed the pounds but the voices remain

"It's just a phase, you'll regain"

My confidence blooms but yet the doubts creeps in

The compliments fade as the negatives whispers spin

My mind is like a battle ground and a raging sea

The echoes of criticism, forever it'll be

I'm trapped in this cycle feeling lost and alone

I'm longing to break free and to call my own

I really want to savor every bite and feel complete

To enjoy my meal without nauseous defeat

To taste and delight without seeing fears dark shade

To simply just eat, be okay and unafraid

But how does okay feel? I've forgotten the way

My mind is drowned by voices, night and day

I try searching for peace and calm within

To silence the echoes so that love can begin

A Heart in Disarray

A marriage is supposed to be a bond that's strong and true

Yet struggles persist and I don't even know what to do

My husband doesn't seem to wanna change his ways

Leaving me uncomfortable, all night and all day

His actions causes a constant source of pain

It makes me question our love all over again

I want to feel safe, to be able to trust and be free

But doubts creeps in a persistent spree

My heart is breaking and my mind in disarray

Overthinking but really not sure what to say

I love him so very deeply, it's so hard to find the strength

To leave and move on to a new length

The image of him with others haunts me so clear

It's a constant reminder of my biggest fear

I want a love where I'm the only one

Where trust and loyalty are never undone

But will I ever find a kind of love so true?

Or am I stuck in the heartache anew?

I want a bond where I'm cherished and adored

Where I'm not left to wonder if I'm being loved or ignored

I'm torn between love and heartache and I know I remain

To long for a relationship that's free from pain

Where our love is pure and trust is the only way

And the hope to feel safe with my partner every single day

Rest in Peace, Auntie

In a room once filled with beautiful light

Now there are shadows in mournful flight

For my beloved aunt who was taken from our sight

Her absence casting solem, endless night

Her voice was a song of joy and light

She had a laugh that soared to celestial hieghts

In her sternness, she had a love that's so pure and deep

She's guiding us with a heart that never sleeps

She was an amazing soul, a beacon of love

She was a mother, daughter, sibling, sent from the stars above

Her spirit will always lingers in the gentle breeze

She's forever a legacy of love that time can not freeze

Although she's gone, her presence will remain strong

In our hearts, she will sing a timeless song

She's an eternal bond that will never depart

My beloved aunt, forever in our hearts

Self Harm

In my dark and restless mind

The thoughts of self harm is a very easy find

A silent battle or the urge to resist

I'm struggling to breathe, it's constant twist

In shadows deep, my thoughts really dwell

Self harm's whisper is a haunting spell

Struggling to resist just to break free

It's all tangled in my thoughts, it really can't simply be

A heavy weight upon my troubled soul

There's an urge to harm but i'm trying not to lose control

Gasping for air in the grip of the night

Finding darkness and seeking the light

But through the storm, I will navigate

Finding the strength in the midst of fate

With each heartbeat, there's a battle cry

I'm resisting the urge, and I'm reaching for the sky

Mentally and Emotionally Tired

The insecurities creeps in like a thief in the night

Stealing my joy and making me question my worth and light

Am I ever gonna be enough? Or Will I ever be?

I'm so tired of trying

And if I'm being honest, I'm really tired of all the lying

I'm dying to find a love that's so true

From someone who's faithful and only wants you too

But the doubt always lingers, it's like a heavy weight

Making me wonder and starting to lose faith

Maybe it really is my fault, maybe I'm to be blamed

For all the pain and heartache and the endless games

I'm so exhausted from all the crying and the bad overthinking too

From the constant feeling used and never feeling new

Whether I'm enough, worthy or loved, it's a constant fight

But I will rise again and shine with all my might

I know I deserve better, I'm beginning to see

That my worth was not destroyed by someone's fleeting glee

I will break free from the tough chains of self doubt, hurt and pain

And I will discover my value, like a sunrise, again and again

THANK YOU LORD

Thank you Lord for this beautiful and brand new day

It came with endless possibilities on the way

The sun is shining and the sky is blue

I'm grateful for being on the wake up list and all the blessings too

I'm extremely thankful for all your love and grace

And for guiding me through life's every race

You gave b=me strength and you keep giving me hope

And with you by my side, I know I will be able to cope

On this beautiful Sunday, I will life up my voice in praise

Because your mercy and kindness has never fades

I am so grateful for this beautiful day that he has made

Because I trust in you to lead me through every shade

So, thank you Lord, for this brand new day

So I can have the chance to live, love and play

May your light shine upon me always

And always guiding me through life's winding ways

TO MY SON

My beautiful little one, my sweetest joy

My love for you can never be destroyed

Because from head to toe, you're pure delight

A precious treasure in my sight

All your giggles, smiles and coos are so dear

It makes my heart sings with countless cheers

With every breath and every beat

I love you a little more, my little sweet

So please continue to be the sweet little boy you are, my darling son

And I know that you will be my only one

The one who fills my life with amazing love and beautiful light

My precious baby boy, you are my heart's delight

Constant Cycle

The beautiful sun is high up in the sky

But yet sleep eludes my weary and watered eyes

My mind is on a constant cycle, it seems

A never ending one that's filled with dreams

I was tossing and turning, trying to rest

But my mind will not obey and I was trying my best

It just keeps on spinning, round and round

It's like sleep is nowhere to be found

As the hours tick and slowly passed by

My chest grows tight, I heave a huge sigh

Then the headache comes, it just feels all too much

I'm so drained and I hate feeling as such

But still, I keep fighting, trying to fall asleep

I counted every sheep and take the leap

I close my eyes, hoping to find

Maybe some peace of mind

Yeah but it's so hard and it's all too tough

When your mind is on an endless cycle, it is rough

But I'm gonna keep trying, I won't give in

Until a peaceful slumber finally wins

My Overthinking

My mind feels like a prison that I can't seem to break free

Overthinking is consuming every single part of me

It's a cycle of worry, doubt and of fear

And it's hard to find happiness when my thought are just so near

I keep replaying conversations and things I've said

I analyze all my actions and all the thoughts in my head

I am trapped in my mind, trying to escape

Overthinking has me in it's tight grip, feels like tape

It keeps killing my happiness and steals my joy

My thoughts feels like a toy that cannot be destroyed

I need a moment just to have some peace and calm

To break free from my mind, feels like a healing balm

But until then I will keep trying to let go

Off the thoughts that weighs me down and just let them flow

I will take a deep breath and try to unwind

And hope that someday, I will find a peace of mind

Anxiety's Grip

Anxiety keeps gripping me so freakin tight

My chest constricts with all it's might

It feels like I am suffocating

Oh man, I really hate this anxious waiting

With each breath I take, feels like a chore

My heart keeps racing, it's a feeling I can't ignore

This feeling just won't go away

I wish... I wish it would just let me stray

But it still lingers, all day and all night

It's a constant battle, a constant fight

I need some peace, for calm and for rest

I want to be free from this anxious test

So I will take a deep breath and try to find ways to cope

With this anxiety, it is hard to elope

I know that I will make it through this test

And find my way to a peaceful rest

My Depression

My depression has drained me, it has left me weak

My tears keeps flowing down my cheek

My mind is trapped in this endless thought

A battle that I have often fought

It has taken everything and more

Left me completely broken on the floor

But still I push on through all the pain

Because my little boy needs me to be sane

Although this life feels like an endless test

I know that I have to do my best

Trying to find ways to heal and cope

And fill my heart with love and hope

So I'm gonna keep fighting, day by day

And even though I might stumble along the way

My love for my little boy will always guide

And help me to find all the strength inside

I'M FOREVER GRATEFUL TO YOU

To my amazing friends, I just want to say

Thank you for being there for me every single day

For accepting me for who I am

And always willing to extend a helping hand

Through thick and thing, you guys have stood by my side

And lifted me up when all I wanted to do was hide

You all have shown me that friendships can be true

And for that, I will forever be grateful to you

Even when I have made mistakes

You guys have never judged me or put me in brakes

You have always been there to see me through

And for that I'll forever be grateful to you

So here's a small poem to express

How much I love each and every one of you, I must confess

You guys are the best friends that a person could find

And for that, I am forever grateful to you in mind

To My Dearest Mother

To my beautiful mother, I just want to say

How much I love and appreciate you more each day

You're the reason I am the person that I am

You're always guiding my through life's every exam

You have been my rock and my shining light

Through my every struggle and my every plight

You've taught me just how to be strong and kind

And how to have an open mind

With all your love and care, I have grown so much

And I have faced life's challenges with a gentle touch

You have shown me what it means to be true

And for that, I'm forever grateful to you

So here's a little poem to express

How much I love you, I gotta confess

You are the reason I am who I am today

And for that, I am forever grateful to you

My Absent Father

My absent father, where have you been?

Your absence left a huge void within

A space that will not be filled

A longing that will not be stilled

Your face and your voice is a distant memory

A yearning for whatever could have been

I'm longing for your love and care

And I just wish that you were ever here

But although you left, I have learned how to cope

And I have found deep within, a huge well of hope

And although you were never there for me

I have grown a lot and have found my destiny

So I'm gonna move on without having regrets

And I'm gonna leave the past without a fret

And although you have been absent on my youth

I have learned to stand and I have found my truth

My Damaged Childhood

My childhood memories are damaged and scarred

A life that was so hard, it left me marred

The pain and the hurt, I wish I could've escape

Haunted me then and it still haunts me today

But although the wounds from my past still remains

I know I don't want to have to bear this pain

For healing can come with the right time and proper care

And I will find the strength to repair

I will face all my demons, one by one

And I will rise above all that has been done

And even though my childhood was torn apart

I will build a strong future with an even stronger heart

So here's to a new day with a fresh start

To healthy healing and hope with a mended heart

I will take all the lesions from my past

And build a future that I know will forever last

TO MY LOVE

To my handsome and loving spouse

I wrote these words within my house

To let you know of my deep affection

And all the joy you bring with your every action

I love your smile, your laugh and your warm embrace

They fill my heart with boundless grace

And in your eyes, I can see a love that's so true

A love that makes my world brand new

Through thick and thin, within every season

Your love will always remain my greatest reason

To face each other, each day filled with hope and cheer

Knowing that with you, I have nothing to fear

So here's to us, my sweet, loving and caring mate

A love that's strong and a love that's great

May we always cherish each other in all our days

And to love each other in countless amount of ways

BROKEN

My heart is so broken and full of pain

The shattered pieces that can't be sustained

The love that you once held and all the many ways you have shed a tear

Is now feeling lost, alone, anxious, worried and filled with fear

But let's not fret, my sweet friend

Because this brokenness is NOT the end

With the right time and care, you will heal again

And love will always come looking for you in the end

So take a deep breath and start over feeling brand new

Let all the hope and light that you have shine through and through

Because even though you're broken, you're going to see

How much stronger and brighter you are going to be

To My Girl

I have never believed in love at first sight

But since I have been talking to this girl, suddenly the sun starts shining really bright

The way she makes me feel all night and all day

Makes me know that she is the one I want and I don't even have to say

I want to keep this one for myself. She's not a secret but I'm keeping her private

Because I know that I want to enjoy this one, I don't want to have to "survive it"

All that I used to beg for, she gives me so far, so effortlessly

I just hope that we will get taken more seriously

I just want to make her happy and show her that she deserves the world and more

Because I feel like she might be the best girl that I've ever asked for

Her beauty is a plus but her personality is top tier

When she calls me "mama", my heart feels safe and have no fears

I want this relationship to work as best as it can

Because she might be my "ONE", I want that to be my ever-lasting plan

So thank you for coming into my life when you did, mamá

Because you are a huge help, healing me from all my trauma

The Name I'll Never Live Up To

My unstable mental health came from my dad

Yeah... idk... maybe I should be glad?

But how could I? When that is all I get to live up to. besides the name

This shows that his family and mine will never be the same

My mom's side of family will always be my number one

Because with them by my side, I have already won

Yes they might have their ways or say the wrong thing

But what better family is there with the goofiness and love that we bring

I will choose being a Denton over being a Sinclair, any day

Because they have stood by my side through everything in every possible way

Honestly, even being a Morris sounds absolutely better

Because my baby boy and I will carry every letter

Social Anxiety

This really isn't a pain that I would wish on anyone

Because it feels like a victory that can never be won

Anxiety and a whole has taken over every part of my life

It's like constantly getting stabbed by Life's wicked knife

I just wanna break free from the chains and bonds of anxiety and just BE!!!

I just wanna stop thinking that the minute I step foot outside, everyone is out to get me

Why is this the only thing I could inherit from my sperm donor?

If I had gotten literally anything else, it would've been such an honor

I find solace in my writing because it's like writing messages that you're never going to send

Because you are so scared of even making yet another friend

Everyone either has failed me or I failed them without realize it

But I will never use someone for my own benefit

The constant breaking down until my tears burn

When is it EVER going to be my turn?

I am tired.... I am getting so exhausted

It is really starting to making me very frustrated

I really hope that one day I'll get to wake up without having to worry about this pain anymore

Because I am tired of having to try and be quiet while crying on the bathroom floor

But until then I'll try to cope in the best way that I possibly can

Even though this was never part of my plan

Rekindling Ties

My big brother and I may not have grown up together

But we have always been there for the time we've known
each other

As kids we were immature on so many levels

But no one could keep us apart, not even the devil

We might not talk everyday and might not be as close

But we are there for each other whenever we need it the most

Our dad may have failed us in more ways than one

But not one of us deserved it, none!!!

I wish my siblings and I could rekindle things

Not being able to know what they're up to, really stings

But hopefully the older we get, the more we'll realize

And start to grow an strong bond which will come to us as a surprise

A Prayer for a Better Year

Thank you Lord for guiding me through this horrible year

Because I could fill a river with every shed of tear

I never want to experience a year like that again

Because all i want is peace and happiness, not lessons and pain

2024 taught me how to be strong, alone

Because I overcome every obstacle that gets thrown

I lived that year in survival mode

And the true color of my closest "friends", really showed

I want 2025 to be an amazing year from January to December

A year that we will always remember

I'm craving a year of loyalty, life and love

That is all I'm asking for, from the Lord above

So let's pray together, for a year filled with success and light

A year that will be worth every fight

A year to be alive and want to stay

So this year has got to be my year even if every day is not my day

A Fragile Heart

I am writing this poem for you

Because I have just realized that there's something I gotta do

I get attached to the first person I find comfort in

And apparently there's an explanation for why that has always been

Everyone I get attached to either leave or die

I don't make friends because I can't handle that loss, no matter how hard I try

When I get attached, I get hurt and I can't handle the kind of pain

Because after what 2024 had put me through, I don't wanna be crying again

But I'm glad I realized it before I get too close to you

Not that you would mind because you just wanna be here for me too

I did it to my big brother and he hated it

He was the only connection I had with my dad and I didn't want to lose it

But with my ex husband, I found comfort in him being my only friend

I never expected us to ever end

I never thought I'd be back here, starting over with someone new

So I got so used to always having him around, I didn't even try to make a few

I'm writing this to explain to you and get you to understand why you became my comfort person

And honestly, I have loved who I am since you became my friend.. I really like this version

But yeah.. it's something I am working on so please be patient with me

I really can't lose this friendship because you are my last missing key

A Cry to be Understood

I just need one person in my life who understands how I really feel

Because no matter how much I try to hide, the feelings started getting a little too real

My mom don't understand but at least she tries to

But I want her to know that I'm not the person she once knew

"You have too much problems, that with you"

That hurts me to core, if only she knew

But I won't tell her because I don't want to hurt her anymore

Because she doesn't deserve that and I still don't love her any less than I did before

She accepts me, just not my lifestyle

And she still gives me everything I need, with a smile

Coming out to her this year was the hardest thing I've ever done

And I feel like I have failed both her and my son

I'm trying, I really am. I just want you to accept me

So that I can finally feel free

Just one person.. who knows how I feel

Because I hate that these feelings are starting to feel too real

FROM PARTNERS TO PARENTS

My ex husband and I are trying to renew our friendship

Since we failed miserably at our relationship

We enjoyed being together for the few good years we got

But man, I'm surprised I survived for all the years we fought

But we are better off as friends

And even though our relationship is over, this is not the end

We still have a handsome baby boy that needs us to be sane

And do whatever we can from all that we gain

This relationship has taught me how to stand alone

And own the crown at my own throne

No one is going to be there for you, so you have to

Because it's time for us to be happy, after all we've been through

So we will keep fighting for this friendship for our son's sake

Because he was never a mistake

We love our baby boy to the moon and back

And even though we're now divorced, we still come in a pack

Protecting My Peace

No one understands how peaceful it feels to be alone

I mean, it is in your own home

I literally avoid social interaction because not everyone is who they seem to be

Besides, I just like to protect my peace and just be feeling free

My home is my safe place

I deserve a place like that, after what I've had to face

I don't even let anyone come over as much

Because I'm genuinely scared of being touched

My family thinks I need to make friends

But when are they gonna understand that I'm living my life for me... when does it end?

The constant force to be an extrovert

I love being who I am, an introvert

I'm not gonna stop being who I am to please anyone

Because after all I survived, I'm finally done

So I want people to stop forcing who they are on me

Because I am not gonna change who I am, never will be

Stepping Into The Unknown

This journey for me will not be easy

And I don't care if that sound cheesy

I am willing to risk it all and to at least try to have a good year

Because I have some amazing people in my life that I know
are going to cheer

I need all the prayers that I can get

Because I have so many wants and needs that have not
been met

My mom, my son, my best guy friend, Joe

These are by far the biggest supporters I know

I just started talking to this girl too

And I don't know, I think she's pretty cool

She has been supporting me since we first crossed paths

And I really want this relationship to be able to last

I think this year will be my best year, yet

And I would lowkey even put that on a bet

Lord, I'm asking you to let this year be good to me

Because there is a big world out there that I would really like
to see

My Sanctuary
Of Work

I love my job, it is the only thing that has kept me sane

It calms everything that goes on in my brain

I am good at my job too

And I enjoy doing what I do

My managers and trainers are the best and they have been there for me

They know my challenges and still manage to be there as much as they can be

I have met some really good friends there too

And they have all supported me, that muchI know is true

It's like my home away from home

Even though I found peace in being alone

I love my job, even though it's hard

And I love the people there that supports me, even when I have us my guard

Instant Connection

I met this amazing friend maybe two months ago

The way how our conversation just flows

It's like we've known each other for years

I feel safe with here, there are little to no fears

She is the best mom that her kids could ever ask for

They are everything to her and more

I lover her kids like they're my own

I just love their presence, even if it's over the phone

I am so proud of her for surviving all she's been through

I hardly tell her but she knows it's true

I'm so glad the day we became friends

And with how much I love this friendship bro, I don't ever want it to end

Love Knows No Bounds

I fell in love with two kids that aren't mine

Nickayla and Ke'mari are so special, really one of a kind

Their mom might be one of the strongest woman I know

Even though she never thinks so

She is doing an amazing job to raise them

Especially given where she's coming from

They are amazing kids, really smart too

Really are their mother's kids, that much I know is true

Being around them, I feel at peace

It's like every pain, they have seized

Especially missing my son, that hurts more than you know

But he'll understand that I did it for him, it'll eventually show

But I am thankful to have met this mom and her amazing little ones

And I pray their light Will shine brighter than the sun's

So I am writing this poem to let them know how much they mean to me

And that's the way it will forever be

FINDING MY VOICE

I always thought singing was my passion

Because I did it despite people's reaction

I still enjoying doing it in my alone time

It was my escape through every mountains I've climbed

But I've found solace in my writing

With every struggles and battles I kept on fighting

This book will be about everything I have been through since I've been a youth

This will be me finally telling my truth

So I'll keep on writing, even with all the haters that may come

Because I have a talent that can help others, better than some

This is what I absolutely love doing

I can't wait till I'll be able to do it under an amazing viewing

A Painful Past

Suicide used to be a constant image in my head

It's like I can never get away, even if I go to bed

I really hated that feeling

It feeling like there was never going to be any healing

I wanted to give up because I was tired of being tired

Tired of feeling excited and uninspired

I just wanted to find a way to shut off my brain

Because I can't take the feeling of this constant pain

But I'm so glad all that is in the past

Even though I really though it was gonna last

I don't write about it because it's painful

I hope you guys understand and don't be too shameful

THE WEIGHT OF SACRIFICE

I love being by myself but sometimes it gets lonely

Because it makes me miss my son, he's my one and only

He's been my only company since the day he was born

And I love being a mother, even though I wasn't warned

I hope to have a relationship that will accept him as their own

Even when he's grown

We come as a package deal

Because he has been my source of strength to heal

I hate what I had to go through to give him the life he has now

Because sometimes I wonder how I made it this long without him, just how

I love my baby boy with everything in me

And I can't believe that my baby boy is about to be three

It has been so hard not being able to see him for this long

And people has been making me feel like this decision I made for him was wrong

But I know that he'll understand that I am doing this for us, one day

And I want him to know that I'm always thinking about him in every way

FALLING FOR YOU

I am so scared to tell this girl how I really feel

Because she might think I'm moving too fast or it's not real

But I don't know how to fake my feelings for someone

And honestly with her, I feel like I've won

It's so easy with her and it's not meant to be that way

But I have found solace in talking to her every single day

I want to use the "L" word so badly but I'm scared of what she might say

Especially if she says nothing, I know my feelings will be hurt in a different way

I really and genuinely like this girl, bro

With her, I'm happy and it's really starting to show

Baby, you're beautiful face is so appealing

I really hope you understand how many parts of me you're healing

I don't think I've ever been with anyone that makes me feel like this

I've become the best version of myself but I have left something for them to miss

But I know that If I do decide to pop out with this one,

Not one of them will be able compare themselves to her, none

Healing Through Creativity

When TikTok came out in 2020

I didn't think it would've become this important to me

I use to drop hints, hoping someone would reach out when I was down

Because my mental health literally had me feeling like I was going to drown

Seeing how many people my contents were helping

Literally has my heart melting

That's why I keep posting, despite the number of views

Or even with the small amount of likes, I refuse

Helping people has always been a dream of mine

Doesn't matter the help, doesn't matter the kind

Black, white, brown, mentally or physically

Especially being able to help them mentally

My contents and poems are my way to heal

And being able to have my poems out there, seems so surreal

But I'm so amazed at how many people I have inspired

Even though most times I'm not always up to it or I'm feeling tired

But I won't stop making contents nor stop writing

Because this is my way of telling you guys to keep on fighting

Because eventually the darkness will end

And the sun will rise again

Six Years Sober

I never thought I'd be a recovering drug addict

But no matter what I tried, I could've never broken that habit

I've been clean now for almost 6 years

And I'm grateful to still be alive because I've cried so many tears

Every line sniffed, every puff

I really thought I was gonna turn out to be a, as Jamaican's say "A cruff"

It hurts knowing I started from such a young age

And it really did send me into a blind rage

I really didn't know how to quit

And trust me everything you can think of, I have tried it

But the highs made me feel safe and forget about all the pain I've been through

Maybe I would've never been an addict if I had another way to cope, if only I knew

But I'm so grateful and happy to still be alive today

To be able to tell my tale and help anyone in any way

Line after line til the bag went dry

If only I loved living like I loved getting high

I'm so thankful that I got clean before I became a mom

Because now I'll get to see him attend his first prom

Out of all my cousins, I'm so glad that I'm the one that went down the wrong path

But on a funny note, all the shit I've been through, I could really use a nice getaway with a bubble bath

The Pain Of Being Undervalued

Can I really trust the people that are close to me?

Because I'm starting to ask myself "who is she?"

I feel like I can hardly find any real friends

Even with the ones who I made amends

I'm not perfect, trust me, I know that

But that doesn't give ppl the excuse to treat me like I'm some kind of bratt

The old me would've found a way to make anything she did, not to be her fault

But the new me actually takes accountability but I still feel, as Jamaicans would say "sack a salt"

I give my everything to people but everyone gives me nothing

And honestly, I would love be given even the smallest thing

"With love", of course but am I really that bad

That not one true friend is yet to be had

This is why I'm so scared of letting anyone get too close to me anymore

Because I actually value myself and my peace a lot now than I have before

So I guess I should be thanking the people that left me when I needed them most

Because if u weren't there for my lows, then u ain't gonna be there for my highs, even if we were extremely close

A Survivor's Story

Every hit, every hair pull, every bite

Felt like I was drawing closer to Life's dangerous knife

I tried getting away, I tried leaving

But she manipulated me and I ended up believing

Domestic Violence is one of the many things I've had to survive from

And all those memories and pain started making me feel numb

The black and blue eyes, the pounding head throb

All the nights I lay there, lying in my own sob

But I'm so grateful to finally be free after going through that for 3 years

And looking back, everything was worth all my many tears

But I would never judge a woman who don't know how to leave

Because I've been that woman but eventually you'll get out, trust and believe

UNSILENCED

"Stop" "I'm just a kid" those were the words I kept screaming

I wanted to wake up from this horrible nightmare because it honestly felt like I was dreaming

Why did he feel like THAT was okay?

Doesn't his conscience bother him to this day

I can't even be with a man sexually without the flashbacks

Those men took everything from me so it was never anything I lack

They took my innocence and my joy along with it

Because feeling them on top of me really made me feel like I wanna commit

I never wanted to be associated with this kind of trauma

Suicide felt like the only way to never have to break the heart of my momma

Sometimes I can feel the pain of them forcing themselves inside me

I was 12 and begging God to take me so I can finally be free

Y'all don't get it, y'all can never understand

How it feels to be a woman who's stuck under a man

Crying as you're fighting, you can't even move his hands

You lay there, crying silently as he's done with his demands

That song is like a replay in my brain

Reminding me of all the agony and pain

Thinking about all the times I had to scrub my skin, makes me shiver

My name is Trisanne Morris and I'm a Sexual Assault SURVIVOR

A Life Of Losses

My dad broke my heart before any man could

Because him leaving me never felt good

I have craved that fatherly love for so long

That all the places I've searched turned out to be so wrong

My innocence was taken from me before I was even a teen

Every wash I wash myself, I just never felt clean

I know I'm beautiful because I've been raped before

That's my way to heal, by using dark humor

When my grandfather died, a small piece of me died with him

It felt like I was drowning but didn't know how to swim

Watching how it broke my aunts, uncles and mom having to lose their father

It is a great deal of pain that I know they wouldn't wish on any other

Losing my favorite cousin was like a stake to the heart

Because he was still so young, I was not ready for him to depart

But I'm so thankful that he's no longer in pain

And one day, I'm hoping to get to see him again

When my childhood best friend stopped talking to me

I just wanted for so long, to just not... BE

I missed her as the years went by

But even though we never saw face to face nor eye to eye

I had a friend that I was trying to get help for

But no matter what I did, she still wanted more

She took her own life because she was mentally unstable

But I did everything I could to take care of her until I was no longer able

When my marriage failed, I was so broken

It felt like all my words felt unspoken

I suffered in silence so that he could be protected

But after all I've had to endure to get here, I know I'll forever be undefeated

When I lost my favorite aunt, I could feel my heart literally breaking in my chest

And I've tried to move on, I've really tried my best

But even thinking about her beautiful face that I won't see anymore

Literally had me crying time and time again, on the floor

All the losses I've had to experience, from one form to the next

I'm surprised I'm still here but I guess I've learnt from the best

Having a strong, black woman for a mother really pays off

And even though I'm better now, I've really had it rough

From Addiction To Recovery

Unless you've been through addiction you do not know how it feels

I had to check myself into a psych

It was my way of coping

I'm clean now and I want to stay that way I am hoping

Every line I sniffed, all my pains start to disappear one by one

I mean, it was temporary but in that moment, I felt ;like this was a victory that can be won

Maybe I didn't want to stop because I hated feeling all those pain

And every time I stopped, "don't stop", "u need this", keeps on replaying in my brain

Withdrawal was the hardest process of quitting

Every shivers, every stomach ache and nausea, I really felt like committing

That would've been my way of not feeling all this pain anymore

And even though I went through all that, I just kept wanting more

If I told you that I didn't miss it, I would be lying

But I choose my sobriety over watching my son crying

Wondering 'why wasn't I good enough to make mommy quit?'

Or when he gets older? "Maybe she being my mom wasn't a good fit?"

Yes the cravings are still there but now I'm better at controlling it

But being sober, feels pretty good, I have to admit

I'm thankful it didn't take my life like it did others

And although I did hurt my mom, I'm so grateful to be alive so that we could be here together

Alone Again

This is why I don't make friends

Because I always fear that it's going to come to an end

I feel at peace when I'm alone

I don't even feel like picking up the phone

Just me, my music and my writing

Because this is the only way I don't have to feel like fighting

I enjoy the few good companies that's been there for me

With them by my side, my spirit is filled with glee

I hate the feeling of being ignored

So I'm looking to you, Lord

Please don't let me lose this one

Being around him, I have so much fun

The way we communicate, be there for each other and vibe

Is the kind of friendship that nobody can describe

It's unique and we like it that way

Even though we don't see each other every day

But right now I feel like I'm this close to losing him

Like me being done with friends, is way too close to the brim

I'm better off alone anyways

And honestly, this is how it's gonna start for the rest of my days

MY BODY, MY CHOICE

Scrubbing my skin till it bleeds

And honestly, I hate where this leads

Unbearable trauma that wasn't my fault

But I'm glad I got through that vault

"Your body, my choice"

But us as women, we need to use our voice

We can't be too quiet anymore

Because we used to have some rights before

This feels like a man's world and we're just living in it

And I hate that feeling, I have to admit

We use our bodies to make a baby from scratch

Well I guess us women are an amazing catch

This is really a trauma that I never wanted to be able to heal from

Because of it, I started feeling dumb

I was hyper sexual but just with females

Because I was genuinely scared of males

But I'm glad I took all the time I needed to heal

Looking back, I never deserved it and I wish it wasn't real

But I'm doing much better now, Thank God

And I'm so much better than being a fraud

Ages Of Agony

I was 11 and wanted to die

I was 16 and the pain got really high

I was 17, with no friends, that made my heart cry

1 was 19 and life didn't feel worth living and I kept wondering why

I was 21 with a heavy heart so deep

I was 23, a young mom and wife with high stress levels and couldn't sleep

I was 24 with a relationship that I tried so hard to keep

I was 25 finally over everything and just wanted to weep

These were all the ages I shouldn't have been here but God saved my life

And I am so grateful to be a mother but I'm so forever thankful that I'm no longer a wife

That relationship drained me along with all the past traumas that I've been through

But I'm in a much better place without him and that much I know is true

Embracing My Introverted Nature

I protect my peace so much, my phone is always dry

And honestly, I just listen my music, write and get high

I'd choose that over being around people any day

Bcz when I was a people person, I got hurt in every single way

I won't let anyone in my space to hurt me like that again

Because my energy? I ain't never gonna let anyone drain

The more I got attached to people, the more I got hurt

And that's why I love being an introvert

If you're in my space, it's because I allow it

But I was never good at making friends anyways so I'm glad that I've quit

I have a huge fear of abandonment because my own dad didn't love me enough when it should've been naturally for him

So I was always asking the question "why would anyone else love me; whether I'm fat or slim?"

But honestly, I don't care if no one loves me now because I love myself

And even though I get made fun of for not being able reaching the top shelf

I enjoy being alone, it's so peaceful

I'm so glad I got to live to feel what this felt like, I'm eternally grateful

Unapologetically Me

No matter what you do in life, someone will always have something to say

Whether you're fat, slim, tall, short... so just live ur life to the fullest every day

You cannot please people, they aren't worth it

Because all they do is use and abuse for their own gain and benefit

So why try to live your life to please them?

They have drained me till I became numb

Now, I love my life for me

And I love the life I'm living, I finally feel free

When I had the weight on, people had something to say

Now, I've lost the weight and people still say something even
to this day

As I said, you can never please people so please yourself

Because now is the time that I'll be taking care of myself

The Guilt Of Joy

I try not to let myself get to happy

Even though my life as I know it, have always been crappy

I feel like when u get too happy, you have a lot more to lose

I don't know if I'm making sense, I don't wanna sound confuse

All I've ever wanted so to be truly happy, no matter how long it takes

But honestly, I think I gave up, with every hurt and betrayal and heartbreaks

I know it sounds crazy but sometimes I feel guilty for how happy I am

And I know I shouldn't be but sometimes life feels like a scam

It's like I want to have a good day but I fear that if I get too happy, something bad is about to happen

And it's like that over and over again

I hate those days where I shut down because of my fears

But I'm eternally grateful for those few people that are always there to wipe my tears

My Peaceful Haven

Man, this girl never seize to amaze me

With her, my heart is filled with glee

She more she treats me well, the harder I fall

And she's always there to answer my every call

Selective Mutism is a symptom of anxiety that I keep quiet

Because with my family, I really didn't wanna start a riot

But I explained it to my girl and she was so patient with me

And for the first time in a long time, my heart finally felt free

My chest started to feel relief just by seeing her, that's how I know she's my peace

But I really home this peace with her do not decrease

And the way she was so calm about it?

It just did everything right there and calmed my spirit

Lost Friendship, Lasting Pain

If I said I don't miss my best friend, I'd be lying

Even though I'm not crying

I took accountability for what I went wrong

And it kills me that I hurt her because she has been my light through my darkness all along

I don't think I'll ever be able to forgive myself got this

Bcz you and I had plans for 2025 that we are going to miss

I didn't only lose you but my son did too

And that's something I really can't believe is really true

But if you're reading this later in life

Just know that losing you hurt so much, it felt like my heart
was stabbed with a knife

I hope that all is well with you

And I hope u survive like you were teaching me to

MY HAPPY PLACE

Being a loner is the best feeling ever

And no matter what anyone says, that won't ever change...
no never!!!

I love to enjoy my own company, that's my peace right there

And honestly, I love not having anyone here

I don't even allow ppl to come to my house anymore

I didn't even used to do that before

I just enjoy being alone

Bcz there's really no greater joy than being home

I love the life I am living now

And I don't want to be unhappy, that I vow

I might not let myself get too happy because of my fears

But I knowI deserve have been through so much and cried so much tears

We Are Somebody

"Your body, my choice",-- those words came from a man

This generation is starting to feel a little too dangerous for a woman

We are used as a therapist, mother and maid

And having to walk on the road feeling scared and afraid

"Not every man is the same" but still almost every woman if not all, have a story

I hate having to walk outside and starting to worry

I don't even like to be touched by a man anymore

Bcz I've had to endure shit from them before and even now

The same man that degrades women, ran straight to a woman for protection!?

How many more women have to go through shit by the hands of men before we take some action?

Actions to make woman feel safe and loved, and not just used as a baby machine

We want to be heard, not just seen

I'm a victim of SA and I'm scared for my life

Because we do our best to be the best mothers and wife

But do we get appreciated for all that we do?

I hate that women are scared to live in a generation like this, if only ppl knew

US women give our everything to a man

Including our bodies, we really thought they were a fan

It's like they only see us as a homebody

We are SOMEBODY, not SOME BODY!!!!

A Tribute To My Therapist

Therapist has been my light throughout my darkness for the past two years

She has been with me through all my shed of tears

She never judge me I made me feel low in anyway

And sometimes I wish I get to talk to her every single day

Even though I get to see her weekly as still, don't feel like that's enough

Because it has helped me to all my times, especially when they are rough

It has been my way of survival

And she's always there to wait upon my arrival

When my work schedule changed, I got worried because I couldn't give up therapy

Is the only thing that makes me really truly happy

Without it, I honestly do not know where I'd be

Because it helped me to embrace to show me

So thank you Mrs. Higgins for all that you have done for me for the time we've known each other

Helping me to get to each bottle without seeming like a bother

You have helped me through my hardest stand, and I am forever grateful

So this is my small appreciation to you to show you how much I am thankful

My Comfort Person

I really don't think this do know how much it means to me

How much being around him, I feel so safe and free

The way he's always there for me when I need him most

And I really love how much our bond is growing close

I want to keep being your friend up to the very end

Because I enjoy every moment with you that I spend

Thank you for being my comfort person, my shoulder to cry on

And I will do not want to hear about my friend being gone

The way you care for me and try to be there for me to my dark times

Even though I feel like I annoy you often times

So, thank you for never giving up on me, neither did you treat me like a bother

And I am happy that we will forever have each other

Protecting My Heart

I don't like being around you because I don't want to hate you

You have done me so much wrongs so I know I should but I grew

You have me my mini best friend

Even though our relationship is over, I do hope our friendship never end

I hope that we remain friends, but from a far

Because you did break me and I still have every scar

Internal scars that I'm trying so hard to heal

And God, I hate how this feel

Even though I love my life now. this was never what I wanted

I started to feel like my whole life was being haunted

You were a crappy husband but you're an amazing dad

And I made sure he got that and even with our friendship
now, I'm glad

Healthy Love, New Beginnings

I have never experienced a healthy relationship

But I have for friendship

I need a love that's real

One that I will always want to feel

I need a love where the loyalty is never undone

Where the love is actual real and this person could be my one

I feel like the girl I'm talking to will be my dream girl

But I know that I'll be trying to give her the world

Having a relationship where we fully trust each other and know that the other won't hurt you

Is a goal of mine that I really want to come through

Tired of crying because I didn't trust when he went out

Because he had filled my mind with so many doubts

So I need a relationship that's peaceful, calm and gentle

One where I won't ever get yelled at because of my mental

One where I'm not being lied to, manipulated and used anymore

Because that is literally all I've been used to from before

Lesson Learnt, Wisdom Gained

I never thought I would've gotten out of the situation that I was in

Now, I'm even happier than I have ever been

I thank God every day for saving my life after those many tries to end it

Because no matter how hard I try, I just did not fit

I tried so hard to fit in until I went with the wrong crowd

It felt so wrong to talk too loud

I love my life now, this freedom and peace I have now, was worth all that pain

But I really can't ever handle going through all that again

I was so drained, it felt exhausted waking up in the morning

But this was a really clear warning

Warning me not to put my all into a person all at once, ever again

Because along with the"love" and "attention", comes hurt and pain

The girl I once was, is definitely not the woman you're reading about today

All that abandonment, pain, betrayal, assaults, and hurt has changed me in every single way

I am wiser, smarter... stronger too

And to all the people that have hurt me, I am so forever thankful to you

By hurting me, it also taught me a lot

With all the many battles I have fought

There was a lesson to be learnt

And now, I don't feel so burt

MY SECOND HOME

My job has become my home away from home

When I'm there, I feel less alone

I don't mind being alone, don't get me wrong

But sometimes it takes courage to have to be strong

This place has become so safe to me

It's the only place besides home, that I feel free

The people I work with are just simply amazing

And I love that even with the smallest accomplishments, they keep on praising

The acknowledge my work and let me know how well I'm doing

I'm good at unloading and doing the floor, it's a whole
viewing

I love my job and I'm really good at what I do

I'm not "full of myself" but that much, I am confident,
is true

MISSING MY SON

I didn't expect being away from my son would've hurt this much

I miss his laughs, smiles, giggles and his tiny touch

I know that I am doing this for the both of us

But I really wish I could take a bus

Baby boy, mommy is doing all she can so you can get the life you deserve

Can't wait until you are old enough to observe

You may have a broken home but you no longer have a broken mother

And together, it'll be us, always, taking care of each other

I can't wait to hold you in my arms again

Because I hate this kind of pain

I'm so sad that you are thriving without me

But I am so proud of the person you are growing up to be

TIKTOK, MY COMMUNITY

TikTok was my way of helping others,

It was a platform where we created a community together.

We got invested in the lives of people we'd never even met,

Forming meaningful connections that flowed effortlessly.

They took away an app that mattered very deeply to us,

Leaving us wondering, "What was the fuss?"

TikTok saved countless lives, that's a fact that's kinda hard to dismiss,

A testament to it's impact, no matter how small it may seem.

This app sparked connections, fostering love and friendships true,

But honestly, it's value extended far beyond, touching lives anew.

Those who took it away will regret their decision, I fear,

And I hope they realize their mistake before it's too late, and there are sheds of tears.

TikTok was important to us, a platform we needed to thrive,

It's absence will be deeply felt, leaving a void that's hard to survive.

I hope that we'll get it back, and this feeling of loss will subside,

For this feels like an attack, leaving our community to hide.

THE PEOPLE WHO HEALED ME

Having people who are real

Are the best thing when you're trying to heal

I love my people, the ones that have been there through my lowest

Even when I have my days when I'm my slowest

These are the people that I'll be taking with me when I'm at my highest

And I'm not gonna ever be biased

These people have been there for me since day one

They have been the community I needed for my son

They have been my light on my darkest days

And to them, I am so grateful in every single way

Thank you guys so much for always being there for me

For me to be comfortable enough and be free

All the support, respect and love

Goes out to you guys, beyond and above

Because it's all you guys have ever given me

So thank you for allowing me to just be

Betrayal Of Trust

I have started seeing the true colors of people I trusted most

They have been there for me and we had gotten so close

They know everything that man put me through

And they sided with him? I still can't believe it's true

Makes me wonder if we were really friends

Or if they knew that our relationship was coming to an end

I really dont have anyone in my life that I can trust

I feel like staying alone at this point, is a must

I'm literally getting so scared of being around anyone

Because I'm the one getting hurt when all is said and done

My traumas literally put fears in my heart

Because I don't think I was always like this from the start

But I guess this is just another lesson I needed to learn

I just keep finding the wrong ones with every turn

But I'm better off alone

Enjoying my own company on my own home

A Labor Of Love

Writing this book has really been a pleasure

It's definitely a moment I'm gonna treasure

Being able to share my story

And doing it without any glory

Just want to help those in need

Because I wished I had this kind of help before I started to bleed

Helping people have always been a passion of mine

It doesn't matter what kind, as long as they were fine

My peaceful music and my led lights

Made writing feel magical, all day and all night

When I tell you the peace I get just locked in my room

But people just gonna wanna assume

I really don't need friends to be happy

Plus, most of who I've come across turned out to be crappy

But I am really loving my life right now

I am hoping for blessings and more

A Heart Once Broken

With every battle I have had to face

I felt like I just couldn't find my place

I really have been through a hell of a lot

And I really did deserve better than I got

My dad was the first man to ever break my heart

I just don't understand why he didn't wanna place his part

I don't hate him but I can never forgive him for what he did

And the worst part is I was just a kid

But I'm happy that I forgave him for me

Just so my mind can finally feel free

Didn't want that trauma bond to ruin anymore relationship

It really made me feel like I'm just a slip

Meaning, maybe I was a mistake

Everything just felt absolutely fake

I know that my mom loves me more than anything

I'm so grateful for her because I hate the hurt that my dad bring

Thank You For The Pain

I don't hate you because I love the woman you made me

I don't hate you because you gave me the opportunity to finally feel free

I don't hate you, even though you made me question everything I thought love was

I don't hate you, even though I wish I knew the cause

I don't hate you because you made me picked up all the pieces that you left me broken with

I don't hate you because I proved to you that I don't need you, never really did

I don't hate you because you gave me my handsome son

I don't hate you because to me, that's a victory won

I don't hate you because you made this heart a little stronger than it was before

I don't hate you because you made me realize that I deserve so much more

I don't hate you even though you made me come undone

I don't hate you because now I get to really find my "One"

So I guess what I'm saying is thank you for all the hurt and pain

It's a great example of what not to do again

It gives me an opportunity to be a better man than you ever will be

And I am so genuinely happy that I get to live out the real ME

A Friendship Lost, But Not Forgotten

Even though my best friend and I aren't friends anymore

I still love her so much, no less than before

I still want what's best for her, she deserves everything good in this life

Even when she becomes someone's wife

She was my light on my darkest days

And I miss her in every single way

Still can't believe she;s not in my 2025

But I am so grateful that she's alive

I hope she reads my book and know how much I miss her

It all still feels like such a blur

But Jay, I hope you're doing well

And just know that you can always ring my cell

Healing A Heart You Didn't Break

You came into my life when I was ready to give up on love

I never wanted to believe father God above

I was tired of getting hurt over and over again

But you're healing a heart that you didn't even break

I am falling harder and harder for you

Something I really never thought I'd have the courage to do

I'm taking a huge risk with my heart right now

And all I want is for someone to love me and more

I have been loving the wrong one for so long

My heart started becoming immune but yet so strong

When I love, I love hard... i'm all in

And since I started talking to you, had been the happiest I've
ever been

I really want this relationship to work

I'm tired of starting over and ending up with jerks

So please, be my "Right One"

Because I feel like together, we'd have so much fun